THE
BIG
TIME

KEVIN DURANT

VALERIE BODDEN

CREATIVE EDUCATION   CREATIVE PAPERBACKS

KEVIN DURANT

TABLE OF CONTENTS

MEET KEVIN

Fans scream and cheer as Kevin catches the basketball. He dribbles down the court. Suddenly, Kevin jumps into the air. He lifts the ball over his head as he flies toward the basket. It's a slam dunk!

Kevin Durant is a star player for the Oklahoma City Thunder. Kevin runs fast, jumps high, and makes amazing shots. Many people think he is one of the best players in the National Basketball Association (NBA).

Kevin dribbles ahead of the defenders to score on a fast break.

KEVIN'S CHILDHOOD

Kevin was born September 29, 1988, in Washington, D.C. He lived with his mom, two brothers, and a sister. Kids sometimes teased Kevin for being too tall.

Kevin's mom goes to as many games as she can.

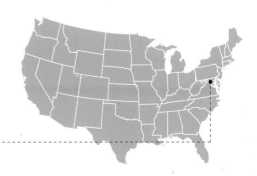

WASHINGTON, D.C.

GETTING INTO BASKETBALL

Kevin started playing basketball when he was eight. Every summer, he spent all day practicing. His team won the national championship two times. Kevin decided he wanted to play in the NBA someday.

Kevin worked hard so that he could make basketball his career, or job.

Kevin was a basketball star in high school. In 2006, he started college at the University of Texas. He played for the school's basketball team, the Longhorns. Kevin won the 2007 Naismith Award as the best player in men's college basketball.

At college, Kevin averaged 25.8 points and 11.1 rebounds each game.

THE BIG TIME

In 2007, Kevin decided to enter the NBA. He was *drafted* by the Seattle SuperSonics. At the end of the season, Kevin was named *Rookie* of the Year.

Kevin was happy to be the second player chosen in the NBA Draft (right).

In 2008, the Seattle SuperSonics became the Oklahoma City Thunder. So Kevin moved to Oklahoma City. From 2010 through 2012, Kevin scored more points per game than any other player in the NBA. In 2012, he won an Olympic gold medal with the United States men's basketball team.

Kevin is 6-foot-9 and weighs 240 pounds.

OFF
THE COURT

When he is not playing basketball, Kevin likes to play video games and shop for clothes. In 2013, Kevin got *engaged* to professional basketball player Monica Wright. Monica plays for the Minnesota Lynx.

Kevin likes going to football games (left) and dressing up for events (right).

WHAT IS NEXT?

In 2012, the Thunder made it to the *NBA Finals*. But they did not win. Kevin hoped to lead his team to a championship someday!

. . . .

In 2014, Kevin won the NBA's Most Valuable Player award.

WHAT KEVIN SAYS ABOUT ...

HIS MOM

"She taught me how to behave on the court and off. She always told me to follow my heart, not to do something just to please someone else."

STAYING HUMBLE

"When people tell me how great I am, I remind myself that I can always be better."

WINNING A CHAMPIONSHIP

"I'm going to take it a day at a time, and you never know what will happen."

GLOSSARY

drafted picked to be on a team; in a sports draft, teams take turns choosing players

engaged promised to get married

NBA Finals a series of games between the NBA's two best teams to see who the champion will be

rookie a player in his first season

READ MORE

Doeden, Matt. *Kevin Durant: Basketball Superstar*. Mankato, Minn.: Capstone, 2012.

Frisch, Aaron. *Oklahoma City Thunder*. Mankato, Minn.: Creative Education, 2012.

WEBSITES

Kevin Durant
http://www.kevindurant.com/
This is Kevin's own site, with lots of pictures and information.

Oklahoma City Thunder: Devon Thunder Kids Club
http://www.nba.com/thunder/fanzone /kids_club_fun_and_games_1011.html
This is the kids' page of Kevin's team, the Oklahoma City Thunder.

INDEX

PUBLISHED BY Creative Education and Creative Paperbacks
P.O. Box 227, Mankato, Minnesota 56002
Creative Education and Creative Paperbacks
are imprints of The Creative Company
www.thecreativecompany.us

DESIGN AND PRODUCTION BY Christine Vanderbeek
PRINTED IN the United States of America

PHOTOGRAPHS BY Alamy (Action Plus Sports Images, epa european pressphoto agency b.v.), Corbis (Steve Boyle, Vernon Bryant/Dallas Morning News, Matt Campbell/epa, Richard Clement/Icon SMI, Jeff Lewis/Icon SMI, Jared McMillen/Aurora Photos, Parisa/Splash News, Tim Sharp/AP, STEVE SISNEY/Reuters, MIKE STONE/Reuters), Dreamstime (Ivicans), Getty Images (Layne Murdoch/NBAE), iStockphoto (Pingebat)

LIBRARY OF CONGRESS CATALOGING-IN-PUBLICATION DATA
Bodden, Valerie.
Kevin Durant / Valerie Bodden.
p. cm. — (The big time)
Includes index.
Summary: An elementary introduction to the life, work, and popularity of Kevin Durant, a professional basketball star for the Oklahoma City Thunder known for being a perennial high scorer.

ISBN 978-1-60818-495-8 (HARDCOVER)
ISBN 978-1-62832-077-0 (PBK)
1. Durant, Kevin, 1988– —Juvenile literature. 2. Basketball players—United States—Biography—Juvenile literature. I. Title.
GV884.D868B64 2014
796.323092—dc23 [B]   2014000249

CCSS: RI.1.1, 2, 3, 4, 5, 6, 7; RI.2.1, 2, 5, 6, 7; RI.3.1, 5, 7, 8; RI.4.3, 5; RF.1.1, 3, 4; RF.2.3, 4

FIRST EDITION
9 8 7 6 5 4 3 2 1

Note: Every effort has been made to ensure that the websites listed above are suitable for children, that they have educational value, and that they contain no inappropriate material. However, because of the nature of the Internet, it is impossible to guarantee that these sites will remain active indefinitely or that their contents will not be altered.